D0907186

Cape Cod Cookbook

Best Recipes from Best Friends

KELLY BALLO MOSS AND MICHAEL BALLO AVILES

This book is dedicated to the memory of our dear mother, Liz Ballo.

Wrinkles will only go where the smiles have been.
Jimmy Buffett

Copyright © 2012 Kelly Moss
All rights reserved. No part of this publication may be reproduced, stored or
transmitted in any form or by any means, electronic, mechanical, photocopying,
recording or otherwise, without the written permission of Kelly Moss.
ISBN-13: 978-0-615-67633-3
Library of Congress Control Number: 2012916212
Additional photo credits:
Page 93 Shutterstock/Otokimus
Page 69 Shutterstock/Luiz Rocha
Page 82 Shutterstock/Anna Hoychuk
Page 140 Shutterstock/Maxfield
www.masarestaurant.com
www.publishatsweetdreams.com
www.kusminarts.com

KAT Designed and produced by Kevin A Trent Limited
www.kevinatrent.com kevin@kevinatrent.com +44 (0)7903 734655

Introduction

Every summer family and friends gather at our beach house to slow down, catch up, eat, laugh and enjoy each others company. As the summers pass we have noticed that everyone, no matter how amateur, has at least ONE great recipe in their repertoire. These are those recipes! Some of them come from Cape Cod. All of them have been brought to Cape Cod. They are as eclectic a bunch as the people who've made them.

Proceeds from the sale of this book will be donated to Spinal Research, a leading charity funding medical research around the world to develop reliable treatments for paralysis caused by a broken back or neck. This organization raises money for clinical treatments as well as vital basic scientific research. Thanks to such pioneering work, paralysis can now be treated and we stand on the brink of applying therapies that will restore movement and feeling and transform the lives of paralyzed people.

The Authors

Kelly Moss and Michael Aviles are sisters who grew up on the beaches of Cape Cod.

After studying and working in floral design, Michael married Chef Philip Aviles and they have a five-year-old son, Palmer. They live in Falmouth, Cape Cod, and Boston, where they own and run a collection of Southwestern restaurants called Masa.

Kelly lives in London with her fourteen-year-old daughter, Chatham. In 2003 she was in a motor vehicle accident in Africa, leaving her a quadriplegic. Kelly has an amazing eye for beauty and continues to develop her artistic talents. Always a fine photographer, she has recently discovered a love of watercolor painting and is currently preparing for her next show.

Kelly likes to hang out in the kitchen and boss people around. Luckily, Michael listens to her and cooks all of the dishes Kelly suggests. They make a perfect team.

Contents

Thirsty

Limoncello

by Suzie Duffy

We are living in a world today where lemonade is made from artificial flavors and furniture polish is made from real lemons.
Alfred E. Newman

Limoncello is Sicily's signature liqueur. Because this distinctive lemon cordial is so easy to make at home it has quickly become a Duffy household name. My favorite time for limoncello is during the holidays. I bottle it and give it as gifts. A perfect way to get someone into the holiday spirit. *Please be advised though if having more than one glass you might consider a designated driver.* Limoncello is also ideal in the heat of the summer. A chilled glass does wonders on a hot sticky day.

Ingredients

The zest of 15 lemons

2 (750ml) bottles of 100 proof vodka or 1 (750ml) bottle of pure grain alcohol

4 cups of granulated sugar

5 cups water

Method

If lemons from Italy are not available, lemons from your local market will do just fine. Choose thick-skinned lemons because they are easier to zest. Wash the lemons with a vegetable brush and hot water to remove any residue. Pat lemons dry. Zest the lemons with a zester or vegetable peeler. Use only the outer part of the rind. Using the pith (white part) of the rind might spoil your limoncello as it is bitter.

In a large glass jar add vodka or, if available, pure grain alcohol. Add the lemon zest. Cover the jar and let sit, preferably in a cool dark place, for at least 30 days. The longer the mixture sits, the better it will be. I give the mixture a quick swirl every other day or so. As the limoncello sits, the alcohol takes on the flavor and yellow color of the lemon zest.

After 30 or so days have passed, combine sugar and water in a medium saucepan. Bring to a boil for 15 minutes or until sugar is completely dissolved; no need to stir.

After the syrup (sugar and water mix) cools to room temperature add to the vodka mixture. Strain the mixture into glass bottles.

Keep in freezer until ready to serve. Salute!

Note: If time permits, after adding the syrup mixture, let that mixture rest for a few weeks before bottling and serving, as I mentioned earlier, the longer the mixture sits, the better the taste will be.

Bourbon Sours

by Karen Lowther

There is no sight on earth more appealing than the sight
of a woman passed out on the bed of the man she loves.

James Lowther

Bourbon + lemon juice + simple syrup = Bourbon Sour

Ingredients

12 oz bourbon

7 oz lime juice

1 cup sugar

1 cup water

Method

To make a simple syrup (make when sober and keep in fridge), dissolve 1 cup granulated sugar in 1 cup of water in a saucepan over low heat, stirring constantly until liquid is clear. Pour into airtight container and place in fridge.

To make the sours, combine bourbon, lemon juice and 2 oz of simple syrup in a blender. While blending, add up to 10 tablespoons of sugar to taste (I like them sour and don't usually add any).

DRINK.

Note: Don't drive. Don't walk. Actually, you can't walk.

Myrtille Vodka

by Robin D'Alessandro

I feel sorry for people who don't drink.
When they wake up in the morning,
that's as good as they're going to feel all day.
Frank Sinatra

Ingredients

8 cups blueberries, rinsed and drained

6 cups of 80 proof vodka

2 cups water

3 cups granulated sugar

4 thin strips lemon peel

Method

Put blueberries in a large glass container or jar and mash them with the back of a wooden spoon. Add alcohol to the berries and stir to mix well. Cover container with lid or airtight wrap and let sit at room temperature or cooler for two weeks. Stir every few days.

After initial aging, strain mixture over a large bowl through a colander or coarse wire mesh strainer. Discard any fruit residue.

Bring 2 cups of water to a boil and pour over sugar and lemon peel. Stir well to completely dissolve sugar. Let cool to room temperature. Remove lemon peel and discard. Clean out container and pour syrup into container adding strained blueberry liquid. Stir to combine. Cap and let age 1½ months or more.

After second aging, strain mixture again through a finer strainer, like a muslin, to remove all sediment. Re-strain as needed until clarity is reached. Bottle and cap as desired. The liqueur may now be used for cooking, but if you are serving as a liqueur, let it age for at least 1 more month. It improves with time.

Sangria

by Ignacio (known as "Nacho")

Nothing ticks me off more than having to fight my way through the fruit to get to the booze – so go easy on the garnish.

Ingredients

2 bottles Spanish Rioja wine

2 cups orange juice

¼ cup sugar

¼ cup brandy

1 oz triple sec

1 quart (2 pints) club soda

2 oranges – cut into eighths and cut each eighth in half

Method

In a big container, mix the oranges, sugar, brandy and orange juice. Mix well to dissolve the sugar and allow to sit for at least 24 hours for the flavors to mellow. "It's important to let it stand," Nacho says.

After 24 hours, add the wine and triple sec and SLOWLY add the club soda, tasting as you go to check the sweetness. There SHOULD be a bit of a liquor bite, but it should NOT be deadly. Likewise it should be sweet but not send you into a diabetic coma. It should also have a decent fizz; if it's too thick, add seltzer (soda water). At this point feel free to add more fruit – diced apples and strawberries are best.

ROUND TRIP
FERRY RATES
CHAPPY FERRY
CAR & DRIVER - $12.00
PASSENGERS - $ 4.00
BIKE & RIDER - $ 6.00
MOPEDS - $ 8.00
MOTORCYCLES - $ 8.00
PAY ON FERRY
COMMUTER BOOKS
AVAILABLE

FREE AREA
MAP

FERRY SCHEDULES
WINTER
OCT. 16 TO MAY 24
DAY - 6:45 AM to 7:30 PM
EVEN. - 9:00 PM to 10:00 PM
11:00 PM to 11:15 PM
SUMMER
MAY 25 TO OCT. 15
6:45 AM to MIDNIGHT
CHECK SCHEDULES WITH CAPT.

PARKING
ONLY

Small Bites

Spanish Tortilla
by Michael Aviles

Also known as Tortilla de Papas, Tortilla Española, Tortilla de Patatas – we just call it delicious!

Ingredients

6 eggs

8 medium-sized potatoes (I like the Yukon Gold)

1 small onion, chopped

¼ cup good olive oil

Kosher salt and pepper to taste

Chopped green onion

Salsa

Sour cream

Method

Preheat oven to 350°F.

Peel and slice potatoes thinly; between ¼ and ⅛ inch wide. Pour the olive oil into a 9–10-inch pan and heat over medium-high heat. Test the temperature of the oil by dropping a slice of potato into the pan. If it starts sizzling the oil is hot enough to start frying the potatoes. Fry potatoes one layer at a time until lightly brown on both sides but not crispy. Transfer with a slotted spoon to paper towel and salt. Work in batches until all the potatoes are done.

Pour out most of the oil from the pan, add the onions and sauté until translucent. When they are done, turn off heat and add potatoes in layers on top of each other.

In mixing bowl beat eggs, salt and pepper. Turn back on heat under pan and pour in the egg mixture. Turn pan side to side to distribute eggs evenly. Let it cook until sides are set. Put in oven at 350°F until eggs are cooked, about 8–12 minutes. Take pan out of oven and flip over onto plate.

Serve with sour cream and chopped green onions or salsa.

Eat warm or at room temperature.

Grilled Halloumi Cheese

by Kelly Moss

What did the cheese say when it looked in the mirror?
Halloumi.

Halloumi is a semi-hard, chewy cheese that comes from Cyprus. It's made from cow's, goat's or sheep's milk, or a combination and has a mild salty flavor. Halloumi has a very high melting point and lends itself beautifully to cooking due to its firm texture, which is retained even when cooked to high temperatures. It's perfect for frying or grilling. It's very popular in Europe and the Middle East and can now be found in many U.S. grocery stores.

Ingredients

¼ lb package of halloumi cheese

3 tbsps olive oil

3 level tbsps flour

3 tbsps extra virgin olive oil

Juice and zest 1 lime

1 heaped tbsp capers, drained

1 tbsp white wine vinegar

1 heaped tbsp grain mustard

1 level tbsp chopped fresh cilantro (coriander) leaves

Method

After you unwrap the halloumi from its vacuum-sealed package, dab it dry with kitchen paper. Using a sharp knife, slice the block of cheese into 8 slices, including the ends, and put aside.

To make the dressing, whisk the lime juice, zest, capers, vinegar, mustard, coriander and olive oil together in a small bowl.

Next, heat the oil in a frying pan over medium heat. When the oil is really hot, press each slice of cheese into flour, seasoned with salt and pepper, to coat it on both sides, then one at a time add them to the hot pan. They take one minute on each side to cook, so by the time the last one's in, it will almost be time to turn the first one over. They need to be a good golden color on each side.

Serve them immediately on a warmed platter with the dressing poured over and garnished with coriander or cilantro. This is good served with lightly toasted pita bread and toasted sesame seeds.

Shrimp Cocktail

by Anne Willis

For a time this appetizer was considered old-fashioned and replaced with trendier fare. However, it seems to be making a well-deserved comeback. In the Willis household, plump, sweet shrimp covered in spicy sauce never went out of style. If you are using frozen shrimp, the safest way to defrost them is in a bowl of ice water in the refrigerator. I like to buy fresh tail-on, peeled, deveined shrimp. Old Bay Seasoning is a famous blend of herbs and spices produced in Maryland specifically to season Chesapeake Bay crabs. Now it's used to add spice to all seafood and meats and can be bought in almost every country.

Ingredients

For the shrimp:

24 extra large tail-on raw shrimp
  (peeled, deveined)

2 tbsps Old Bay Seasoning

1 lemon, halved

1 tsp finely minced garlic

1 clove garlic, finely minced

½ tsp chili powder

1 bay leaf

1 tsp salt

For the cocktail sauce:

2 tbsps chili sauce

1 cup ketchup

1 tbsp horseradish

1 dash Worcestershire sauce

Juice of ½ lemon

½ tsp Tabasco

½ clove garlic, finely minced

1 tbsp cilantro (coriander) chopped

Method

To prepare the cocktail sauce, mix all the cocktail sauce ingredients together in a medium bowl and refrigerate until ready to serve.

Have a large bowl of ice water ready and set near the sink. Fill a large stockpot with water, add the Old Bay, lemon, granulated garlic, garlic, bay leaf, chili powder, and salt. Bring water to a boil. Add the shrimp to the pot and when the water returns to a boil, the shrimp should be done. The shrimp should be bright pink. This will only take a few minutes.

Immediately drain and place the shrimp in the ice bath for 2 minutes to cool.

Drain and serve with the cocktail sauce.

Lobster Bisque

by Nick Moore

Obviously, the main ingredient of this recipe is lobster. I tend to use leftover lobster. Although, anyone who has eaten with my family will realize the term "leftover lobster" is an oxymoron. Be sneaky – cook two extra lobsters. Let them cool and hide them in the fridge (behind the fruit and vegetables – no one will look there) and make the bisque the next day.

Ingredients

2–3 1 lb lobsters

5 tbsps extra virgin olive oil

5 tbsps unsalted butter

2 leeks, halved lengthwise

2 onions chopped

2 stalks celery, chopped into big chunks

2 carrots, chopped into big chunks

1 tbsp garlic, minced

6 sprigs fresh thyme

2 tbsps tomato paste

½ cup cognac

½ cup sherry

3 tbsps all-purpose flour

4 cups heavy (double) cream

Cayenne pepper

Kosher salt and freshly ground black pepper

Paprika, optional

Method

Remove meat from cooked lobsters and put aside. Remove brain sac and liver from lobster shells and throw away. Retain any juices.

Heat 3 tablespoons olive oil in a large pot over medium heat and melt 3 tablespoons of butter in it. Add the lobster bodies and heads and their juices, the leeks, garlic, one chopped onion, celery, carrots, half the thyme and the tomato paste. Use a whisk to break up the tomato paste. Cook until the shells are warmed and the vegetables are soft, about 10–15 minutes.

Next, pour in half the cognac and the sherry and let the alcohol burn off. Sprinkle in the flour, stir and cook for another 2 minutes. Add water to cover and stir up all the browned bits on the bottom of the pot with the whisk. As soon as it boils decrease the heat and gently simmer until the stock is reduced and thickened, about 30–45 minutes. Strain this into a clean pot and season with salt and pepper if needed; add the cream, a pinch of cayenne pepper and let simmer for 5–10 minutes. Take off heat and put aside.

In a sauté pan, heat the remaining 2 tablespoons olive oil and 2 tablespoons butter over medium heat. Add remaining onion, thyme, and bay leaf, and let this mixture cook for about 5 minutes. Add the leftover lobster meat, roughly chopped. Pour in the remaining ¼ cup Cognac and let the alcohol burn off. Cook for a few minutes to flavor and warm the lobster pieces, then remove the lobster and set aside. Reheat the strained bisque and add the lobster pieces. Sprinkle bisque with a dash of paprika, if using, and serve.

Grilled Stuffed Squid

by Cutter Colby

In the sagas of undersea outlaws,
And the great soggy deeds that they did,
The saltiest thief ever swam down a reef
Was an outlaw named Billy the Squid.

"Billy the Squid", Tom Chapin and John Forster (1992)

Ingredients

¾ cup fine fresh bread crumbs

⅓ cup whole milk

¾ tsp fennel seeds

½ lb ground pork

2 large garlic cloves, minced

1 heaped tbsp capers
(preferably salt-packed)

¼ tsp paprika

12 cleaned small (3–4-inch) squid bodies
plus tentacles (about 1 lb total)

3 tbsps extra virgin olive oil
plus additional for drizzling

1 tbsp chopped fresh dill

½ tsp Tabasco sauce

Method

If you're using salty capers, rinse the capers, soak in cold water for 10 minutes, then rinse again. Soak breadcrumbs in milk in a large bowl.

Toast fennel seeds in a dry small skillet (not non-stick) over medium–low heat, shaking skillet occasionally, until fragrant, 3–4 minutes. Chop fennel seeds and add to breadcrumb mixture along with pork, garlic, paprika, Tabasco, chopped capers, parsley, ½ teaspoon salt, and ¼ teaspoon pepper. Gently mix with your hands until well blended. Remove tentacles from squid bodies and reserve. Using a small spoon, loosely stuff squid with pork mixture, leaving a ½-inch space at top (you may have some stuffing left over). Seal tops using toothpicks.

If you are cooking on an outdoor grill, get the charcoal hot first and ready to cook. If you're cooking on the stove, use medium heat and use a grill pan so you get nice grill lines on the squid. Coat stuffed squid bodies and tentacles with olive oil and season with salt. Oil grill rack, or pan, and then grill stuffed squid, turning frequently, until golden in spots. If you have an instant-read thermometer, insert it into center of filling. When it reads 150–155°F, they are done. This should take 12–15 minutes. Transfer to a platter. Grill tentacles until opaque and curled, about 1 minute, then add to platter. Drizzle with oil, sprinkle with dill and serve with lemon wedges.

Zucchini and Feta Fritters

by Skipper

These are a delicious summertime treat. Zucchinis don't have much flavor but the salty feta makes up for it. They make a great hors d'oeuvre and are best served immediately after cooking, while still hot and crispy.

Ingredients

2 lbs zucchini, grated

Freshly ground black pepper

Bunch spring onion, white part chopped, the green part discarded

2 tbsps dill, chopped

2 tbsps flat-leaf parsley, chopped

3 free-range eggs

1 tbsp paprika

8 oz feta cheese

8 oz plain flour

Groundnut oil, for deep frying

Slices lemon, to garnish

Method

Sprinkle the zucchini with salt and allow to drain in a colander for 20 minutes.

Place the grated zucchini into a clean kitchen towel and squeeze out the water. Mix with the onions, dill, parsley, eggs, paprika and freshly ground black pepper. Work in the feta cheese and flour.

Heat the oil in a deep, heavy-bottomed pan. You will know it's ready when a breadcrumb that is dropped in will sizzle gently in it.

Carefully drop 1 heaped tablespoon of the mixture in the hot oil and flatten slightly. Fry for about 2 minutes on each side or until golden. Remove with a slotted spoon and drain on paper towels. Garnish with slices of lemon and serve immediately.

Sizzling Prawns

by Caroline Sainsot

These are great as a nibble during a prolonged cocktail hour, not that anyone can remember having nibbled them.

Ingredients

Juice of 2 limes

2 cloves garlic, minced

1 small green chili, deseeded and finely chopped

1 inch piece of ginger, grated

½ tsp turmeric

1 lb raw king prawns, peeled and deveined

3 tbsps cornstarch (cornflour)

6 tbsps of sunflower oil

1½ tbsps coriander, chopped

Method

Mix lime juice, garlic, chili, ginger and turmeric in a large bowl and leave aside to marry the flavors together.

Pat prawns dry with kitchen paper and place in lime juice marinade – cover and chill for 30 minutes.

Sift cornstarch onto a large plate. Add half of the prawns to the cornstarch and coat lightly. Heat 3 tablespoons of oil in large frying pan on medium heat and fry coated prawns for about 3 minutes turning occasionally, until just cooked and crisp. Drain on kitchen paper and cover with foil to keep warm. Coat the remaining prawns and fry in remaining oil.

Garnish with coriander and serve immediately with extra lime wedges and a sprinkling of sea salt.

Clams Casino

by James Lowther

James doesn't actually make this clam recipe. He would but he's too busy breaking things at the beach house, like the shower, the toilet, the curtain rods – BUT, he does go out with his buddy Mike and "rake" the sand bars for our clams. It's a laborious job, especially for James as he doesn't even like clams.

Ingredients

32 littleneck clams on the half shell

¼ lb bacon, finely diced

6 cloves garlic, finely chopped

½ tsp hot pepper flakes

2 tbsps extra virgin olive oil

2 tbsps finely chopped flat-leaf parsley

½ cup fresh bread crumbs

Freshly ground black pepper

Method

Preheat broiler to high.

Place a medium sauté pan over medium-high heat, add the bacon and cook until lightly golden-brown. Add the garlic and red pepper flakes and continue cooking until the bacon is crisp. Remove from the heat, stir in the olive oil, parsley and bread crumbs and season with black pepper, to taste.

Open clams and top with bacon mixture and place under the broiler. Broil for about 1 minute or until just cooked through. Serve immediately.

Falafel with Garlicky Tahini Sauce

by Said

OK, this guy, Said, never came to the beach house BUT when driving us around Israel, he pulled over by the Dead Sea and whipped up these falafels using his family's recipe. Awesome!

Ingredients

For the tahini sauce:

1 cup tahini (sesame seed paste)

½ cup canned chickpeas, drained and rinsed

1 lemon, juiced

2 garlic cloves, chopped

1¼ tspss kosher salt

½ tsp cayenne pepper

For the falafel:

½ cup canned chickpeas, drained

¾ lb ground lamb

3 tbsps green onions, white and light-green parts only, finely chopped

2 garlic cloves, finely chopped

½ cup finely chopped fresh cilantro (coriander)

¼ cup finely chopped fresh parsley

1 tsp kosher salt

1 tsp ground coriander

1 tsp ground cumin

½ tsp ground black pepper

Large pinch cayenne

½ cup olive oil

Method

To make the sauce, combine ingredients in a food processor. As you purée, add ½ to ¾ cup of water through feed tube until mixture is smooth. Taste and adjust seasoning if necessary. Sauce should be thinner than hummus. Tahini is a Middle Eastern sesame seed paste you can now find in most grocery stores.

For the balls, in a large bowl, mash ½ cup chickpeas with a potato masher or fork. Add remaining ingredients and mix well with your hands or a wooden spoon. Form into 1 ¼-inch balls.

Heat oil in a large skillet over medium-high heat until shimmering. Cook balls in batches, turning occasionally until golden-brown all over and just cooked through, 5–6 minutes. Transfer to a plate lined with paper towels. Drizzle with sauce and serve immediately.

Serves 3–4

Barley and Sausage Soup

by Terri DiGiovanni

Soup is just a way of screwing you out of a meal.

Jay Leno

Ingredients

5 tbsps extra virgin olive oil

1 large onion, chopped

2 small carrots, cubed

½ celery stalk, chopped

3 garlic cloves, chopped

1 cup barley

3 tbsps flat-leaf parsley, chopped

1½ quarts (3 pints) chicken broth

¼ tsp dried oregano

¼ tsp fresh rosemary

Kosher salt to taste

Freshly ground black pepper

8 oz Italian sausage, without casing, cut into ½-inch pieces*

1 medium all-purpose potato or red potato, cubed

Method

In a large stockpot, heat 3 tbsps olive oil over medium heat. Add the onion and cook, stirring frequently until lightly brown, about 10 minutes. Add the carrots, celery and garlic. Stir and cook another 3–4 minutes. Add the barley, parsley, chicken broth, oregano, rosemary and salt and pepper to taste. After bringing to a boil, reduce heat to a simmer and cook for about 30 minutes.

In the meantime, heat 2 tablespoons olive oil in sauté pan over medium heat. Add the sausage and cook until nicely brown, approximately 6–8 minutes. When done, remove sausage from pan and set aside on paper towels. Add the sausage and the potato to the soup and simmer for an additional 20 minutes or until the potatoes are tender. Check the seasoning… THE SOUP SHOULD BE PEPPERY. If too thick, add more broth.

*A TERRI TIP!!! I use "HOT" Italian turkey sausage for more flavor and less fat.

Gazpacho

by Julie Sullivan

'I didn't care much for the gazpacho soup.
I mean where's the fun of sending it back because it isn't hot?'
Colleen, *30 Rock*

Ingredients

1–2 English cucumbers, diced into ½-inch cubes

2–3 lbs large tomatoes, diced (squeeze before dicing to remove seeds)

2 red peppers, chopped

1 red onion, diced

3 garlic cloves, minced

¼ cup sherry wine vinegar

1 can (24oz) of crushed tomatoes (only needed if fresh tomatoes are out of season)

Salt and pepper

¼ cup fresh parsley, chopped

¼ cup fresh basil, chopped

Juice of 1 lime

Dash of Tabasco

Croutons:

Crusty French baguette or ciabatta loaf

Olive oil

Grated parmesan cheese

Crushed sea salt

Pepper

Smoked paprika

¼ cup parsley, chopped

Method

In large bowl combine vegetables and stir in salt and vinegar; if time permits, let this mixture sit for half an hour. Add remaining ingredients and mix well. If you don't like it chunky, add half the mixture to a food processor or blender and blend until smooth. Combine the blended veggies with original mixture. If you are making with supermarket tomatoes you may need to cheat a little with the 24 oz can of crushed tomatoes (Pastene or Redpack) as the out-of-season ones are much less juicy than fresh local ones. (If you want to be totally lazy you can use all canned crushed tomatoes, I won't tell.)

Chill for 4 hours and serve with accoutrements of chopped cucumber, onion, pepper, croutons, and top with a teaspoon of the sherry vinegar. If you are making on the fly, you can add a few ice cubes into the mixture to quicken the chill but not too many or it will be watery!

Preheat oven to 450°F.

Take a small thin baguette or ciabatta loaf and cut into 1-inch cubes. This is even better if you leave the bread out overnight to get just a bit stale. Put the cubes into a large bowl and drizzle with olive oil and toss with your hands. Then season with salt and pepper and toss again. Follow with the parsley and toss again. The cubes should be coated, not sopping with oil. Spread on a parchment paper lined baking sheet and sprinkle with cheese. Bake at 450°F for about 10–12 minutes, turning half way through and sprinkling cheese again on the other side. When nice and golden, remove and let cool for a minute. Get a clean paper bag and put about 2–3 tablespoons of the coarse salt and a teaspoon of the paprika inside the bag. Put the croutons in the bag, fold up and give a good shake! Serve alongside your delicious gazpacho!

New England Clam Chowder

by Miles Standish

But when that smoking chowder came in, the mystery was delightfully explained. Oh! Sweet friends, hearken to me. It was made of small juicy clams, scarcely bigger than hazel nuts, mixed with pounded ship biscuits and salted pork cut up into little flakes! the whole enriched with butter, and plentifully seasoned with pepper and salt – we dispatched it with great expedition.

Moby-Dick – Herman Melville (1851)

Ingredients

2 tsps vegetable oil

4 slices chopped salt pork (you can substitute bacon or pancetta)

1 medium onion, chopped

2 celery stalks, chopped

2 tsps chopped fresh thyme, or 1 tsp dried

1 medium red potato, diced

8 oz bottled clam juice

1 bay leaf

3 cups low-fat milk

½ cup heavy (double) cream

⅓ cup all-purpose flour

¾ tsp salt

12 oz fresh clams, chopped (you can use canned clams)

Parsley, finely chopped

Tabasco

Method

Heat the oil in a large saucepan over medium heat. Add salt pork and cook until almost crispy, 4–6 minutes. Add onion, celery and thyme to the pan; cook, stirring, until beginning to soften, about 2 minutes. Add diced potato, clam juice and bay leaf. Bring to a simmer, cover and cook until the vegetables are just tender, 8–10 minutes.

Whisk milk, cream, flour and salt in a medium bowl. Add to the pan and return to a simmer, stirring, over medium-high heat. Cook, stirring, until thickened; about 2 minutes. Add clams and a few dashes of Tabasco and cook, stirring occasionally, until the clams are just cooked through, about 3 minutes more. Discard bay leaf.

Ladle into bowls and top each serving with oyster crackers and parsley or scallions.

Barbequed Artichokes

by Nonna Rosa

*If God had intended for us to follow recipes,
He wouldn't have given us grandmothers.*
Linda Henley

Margo's mother-in-law lives in Naples, Italy and makes these every time they are in season. These really do need to be cooked on a barbeque but my God are they good!

Ingredients

10 small artichokes

10 cloves garlic, thickly sliced

Salt

Pepper

Olive oil

½ cup fresh parsley, chopped

Method

In a bowl, mix the parsley, garlic, salt and pepper. Drizzle in the olive oil until the mixture has a pasty consistency, probably 2–3 tablespoons. Cut the stems off the artichokes. Stuff the insides of the artichokes with the mixture, making sure to get in between all the leaves and coating tops and bottoms of the leaves. Don't bother putting it between the outer leaves because when you barbecue them all the outer leaves will be burnt.

Once stuffed, place them all on the barbecue and allow them to cook for at least 30–45 minutes. Don't worry if they look burnt. Once cooked, remove and let them cool. Peel away all the burnt leaves and leave the inner ones. The garlic, parsley and olive oil will have soaked into the artichoke and the barbecue will give it a smoked flavor. Delicious!

Chorizo and Chickpea Stew

by Judy Bernard

What is a chickpea if it's neither a chick nor a pea?

Ingredients

2 15 oz cans chickpeas in water, drained

½ lb chorizo, sliced into bite-size pieces

1 medium onion, finely chopped

2 sticks celery, finely chopped

2 cloves garlic, chopped

1 bay leaf

1 tsp paprika

⅔ cup dry white wine

15 oz can plum tomatoes

Small bunch parsley, chopped

Method

Fry the chorizo in a large, non-stick frying pan until it releases its oil. Add the onion, celery and garlic and cook until softened.

Add the wine, tomatoes, bay leaf, paprika and seasoning to the pan and simmer for 15 minutes, stirring occasionally to break up the tomatoes, until the sauce has thickened.

Stir in the chickpeas and simmer for another 5 minutes. Check seasoning, then garnish with chopped flat-leaf parsley and serve with a salad and crusty bread to mop up.

Lamb Nachos

by Palmer Aviles

Kids love these and they are so much healthier than corn chips with mysterious melted yellow cheese!

Ingredients

5 pita breads, cut into wedges

4 oz feta cheese

½ cup yogurt, plain Greek-style

½ cup chopped fresh mint

1 lemon

1 medium onion, chopped

½ lb ground lamb

1 tbsp ground cumin

½ tbsp dried oregano

2 or 3 medium ripe tomatoes, chopped

1 medium cucumber, peeled, seeded, and chopped

½ cup black olives, pitted and halved

About ½ cup olive oil

¼ cup pine nuts (optional)

Salt and freshly ground pepper

Method

Heat oven to 350°F. Arrange pita wedges in one layer on baking sheets and drizzle with a tablespoon or two of olive oil. Use your hands to mix up until all the pieces are lightly covered in oil. Bake until they begin to color, turning once or twice, about 10 minutes. Sprinkle with salt, turn off oven and put chips back in to keep warm. While the pitas cook, put the pine nuts in a dry, non-stick pan and toast. This won't take long, so keep an eye on them and shake constantly.

In a blender or food processor, combine feta, yogurt, ¼ cup olive oil, mint and zest and juice of lemon; sprinkle with salt and pepper. Blend until smooth. You can also mash mixture by hand, with a fork.

Put 2 tablespoons of oil in a skillet over medium-high heat and cook onions until soft, about 5 minutes. Add lamb, cumin, oregano, salt and pepper; continue cooking until meat is cooked through, about 5–10 minutes more.

Put chips on a serving plate and top with lamb, feta sauce, tomatoes, cucumbers, olives and pine nuts if you're using them.

Full Bites

New Orleans Shrimp and Chicken Jambalaya

by "Tiny" Whittington

Jambalaya and a crawfish pie and fillet gumbo
Cause tonight I'm gonna see my ma cher amio.

"Jambalaya on the Bayou," The Carpenters

Ingredients

1 tbsp unsalted butter

½ cup Andouille sausage (any spicy sausage will do, we use chorizo), diced

½ cup onion, diced

½ cup bell pepper, diced

½ cup celery, diced

½ cup fresh tomatoes, diced

½ cup tomato sauce

¾ cup long-grain rice

1½ cup chicken stock

2 tbsps garlic, minced

1 tbsp Worcestershire sauce

½ cup raw chicken, diced

1½ cup medium shrimps or prawns

1 tbsp fresh parsley, chopped

3 tbsps green onions (scallions), chopped

¼ tsp cayenne pepper

1 tsp freshly ground pepper

½ tsp dried thyme

½ tsp dried basil

½ tsp dried sage, chopped

1 tsp kosher salt

Method

Preheat the oven to 350°F.

Mix together the onion, celery, and bell pepper. In Cajun cooking this is called the Holy Trinity and is the base for much of the cooking in traditional Louisiana dishes.

In a cast-iron Dutch Oven or other ovenproof pot, melt the butter over medium heat, add the sausage and cook until it just starts to brown. Add half of the Holy Trinity, cook until the vegetables are tender. Add the diced tomatoes and cook for 1 minute. Add the tomato sauce and cook for another minute. Add the rice and cook for 2 minutes, stirring constantly. Add the stock, the other half of the Holy Trinity, cayenne pepper, ground pepper, salt, thyme, sage, basil, Worcestershire, and the garlic. Taste the broth for seasoning, particularly salt. Add the chicken, stir well and put the pot in the preheated oven. Bake uncovered for 25 minutes.

After the 25 minutes, stir in the raw shrimp, parsley, and green onions, cover and place back in the oven for an additional 10 minutes, or until the shrimps are cooked through. At this point you might want to check whether the mixture needs more liquid and add more stock if necessary.

This serves 3–4 people so you may want to double it.

Farfalle alla Vodka
(Bow Tie Pasta with Vodka Sauce)

by Benedetta Casini

According to Benedetta, ALL the best cooks come from Northern Italy! In her pasta sauce, the salty flavor of the pancetta, the richness of the cream and the sweetness of the tomatoes are a perfect combination that has become a tradition in every Italian restaurant.

You can use bacon but then it's a whole different recipe and, to be honest, it's worth the trip to the Italian grocer to pick up pancetta.

Ingredients

1 lb of farfalle pasta

1 cup tomato sauce, pureed

6 slices of pancetta (unsmoked), you can substitute bacon

½ white onion

½ red chili pepper, minced, no seeds

Handful of basil leaves, chopped

½ cup vodka

¾ cup light (single) cream

Extra virgin olive oil

Grated parmesan cheese

Method

Finely chop the onion and the pancetta. Gently fry both of them in 3 tablespoons of extra virgin olive oil on moderate heat. Add the chili pepper according to taste. Add the tomato sauce and the chopped basil leaves and gently cook for 5 minutes. Add half of the vodka and keep cooking in moderate heat until it evaporates completely. Pour in the light cream until the sauce becomes pink.

Bring a large pot of water to boil, add a dash of salt. Cook pasta for a few minutes, until it's al dente. I usually find to get al dente pasta you should cook the pasta 1 minute less than it says on the package.

Combine cooked pasta and sauce. Adjust salt and pepper. Sprinkle with grated parmesan.

Drink the other half of the glass of vodka and enjoy!

Macaroni and Cheese

by Liza Miller

*The poets have been mysteriously silent
on the subject of cheese.*

G.K. Chesterton

Ingredients

1 lb large elbow macaroni cooked al dente and drained

For the sauce:

6 tbsps butter

3 oz flour

3 cups cold milk

1 cup heavy (double) cream

1 tsp salt

1 tsp black pepper

1 lb white Vermont cheddar, shredded

4 oz Romano cheese, shredded

4 oz Asiago cheese, shredded

For the topping:

2 cups Panko bread crumbs (or substitute regular breadcrumbs)

8 tbsps butter, melted

Method

To make the sauce:

In a large saucepan, melt the butter. Add the flour and cook, stirring for 2–3 minutes on medium heat. Add the milk and whisk vigorously until dissolved. Cook on medium heat until thick and bubbly. Add heavy (double) cream, cheddar, Romano, Asiago, salt and pepper. Cook until the cheeses melt.

Add cooked macaroni and mix well. Transfer mixture to a medium-size baking dish.

To make the topping:

Mix together Panko and melted butter. Sprinkle on top of macaroni mixture.

Bake at 325˚F for 15 minutes or until golden.

Lobster Roll

by Christopher Alden

Lobster, mayonnaise and bread – really?! If anyone can come up with a better combination, I'd like to hear it. If you really want to knock yourself out (and by "knock yourself out" I mean slowly kill yourself) then slab a little butter and garlic on the roll and grill it before you stuff it with lobster. Obviously, the lettuce will help ease your conscience.

Ingredients

1½ lbs cooked and cubed lobster meat

4 hotdog buns or Kaiser rolls, split

4 lettuce leaves

2 tbsps mayonnaise

1 tsp fresh lime juice

1 dash hot pepper sauce (e.g., Tabasco)

2 green onions, chopped

1 stalk celery, finely chopped

Salt and pepper to taste

1 pinch dried basil, parsley or tarragon

Method

In a medium bowl, stir together the mayonnaise, lime juice, hot pepper sauce, salt and pepper until well blended. Mix in the green onion and celery, and then lightly mix in the lobster so it just gets coated without falling apart.

Stuff the lobster filling into the buns with a lettuce leaf each and sprinkle parsley, basil or tarragon lightly over the filling.

Rack of Lamb with Herb Crust

by Uncle Frank

1 rack of lamb, 1½–2 lbs, French-trimmed

4 tbsps olive oil

4 cloves of garlic, peeled and smashed

3 tbsps fresh rosemary, chopped

¼ cup parsley, chopped

½ tsp Tabasco sauce

½ tsp Worchestershire sauce

½ cup of whole-grain mustard

¼ cup of bread crumbs

Dash of paprika

Method

Prepare lamb. Usually when you buy a rack of lamb it has already been trimmed so the rib bones are exposed. If not, remove most of the fat from the back of the rack. Leave a little to flavor the meat as it cooks. Then French-trim the bones by cutting the fat out around each bone down to the meat. Scrape the bones of all sinew and fat. Next, score the fat, by making sharp shallow cuts through the fat, spaced about an inch apart. Season lamb very well with salt and pepper.

In a bowl, mix all ingredients together to form a herb paste. Then firmly pack the paste all over the rack and let marinate in the fridge for 1–2 hours.

Preheat the oven at 400°F and while it's getting hot, take the lamb from the fridge. Leave it for 20 minutes or so until it comes to room temperature.

Place roast in middle of a roasting pan (fat side up) and wrap a little foil on the exposed ribs so they don't burn. Cook in the oven at 400°F for 10–15 minutes for pink to medium. It's ready when a meat thermometer inserted into the thickest part of the meat reads 125°F for rare or 135°F for medium. When ready, remove from oven, cover with foil and let rest for 5–10 minutes.

Cut lamb chops away from the rack by slicing between the bones.

Serves 2–3

Penne with Swordfish

"Penne con pesce spada di nonna Marina"

by Simonetta Pozzi

The fishing was good, it was the catching that was bad.
Ernest Hemingway

Here's a trick that almost every Italian seems to know but rarely shares! After you boil pasta but before you drain it, reserve a bit of the water it cooked in to add to any sauce you're making. Stir a few tablespoons at a time into your simmering sauce. The sauce will thin out a little and then thicken as the starchy water is absorbed. It feels counter-intuitive to add water to a sauce in order to thicken it, but a little starchy cooking water gives the sauce extra body and an almost creamy texture.

Ingredients

1 small onion (or a half a medium one)

1 garlic clove

½ lb swordfish

2 cups cherry tomatoes, cut in half

3 heaped tbsps capers

Basil, chopped

Parsley, chopped

Extra virgin olive oil

Chili flakes

1 lb penne pasta

Salt and pepper

Method

Wash and drain the capers (the best ones are Italian, salted ones). Very finely chop the onion and garlic, and dice the swordfish into small bite-size pieces.

In a pan, sauté the onion and garlic in 3–4 tbsps oil; cook slowly until soft and golden in color. Turn the heat higher and add the swordfish.

When the fish seems almost ready (it should still be pink in the middle), add the cherry tomatoes, with the capers, salt, pepper and a pinch of chili flakes. Cook for 5–7 minutes.

At the last minute add parsley and basil, which has been very finely chopped.

Cook the pasta al dente and add to the sauce (save some water that the pasta cooked in to add to the sauce if it's too dry).

Serve immediately.

Serves 4

Crab Cakes

by Ray and Jane Derman

Ingredients

1 lb crabmeat

¼ stick butter (2oz)

1 grated small onion

3 tbsps flour

¾ cup heavy (double) cream

1 tbsp chopped parsley

2 cloves minced garlic

1 tsp Worcestershire sauce

½ tsp powdered mustard

2 egg yolks

2 dashes Tabasco

Salt and pepper

1 beaten egg, for dipping

Good bread crumbs

Method

Pick through the crabmeat removing the tiny bits of shell. I guarantee you'll find some. Try not to break up the lumps of crab too much.

Melt the butter in a heavy skillet, and cook the onion, parsley and garlic until translucent.

Mix the cream with the Worcestershire sauce, mustard, egg yolks, Tabasco, salt and pepper.

Stir the mixture into the skillet and mix well, cooking and stirring a short while longer.

Add the crabmeat and GENTLY stir in so as not to break it up. Remove from heat.

Put the mixture in the fridge for a couple of hours until it cools. After the mixture cools, it will be firm and easier to shape it into small cakes. Once the cakes are formed, dip them in the beaten egg mixture and then gently roll in breadcrumbs. Fry in butter until slightly browned – don't overcook.

Eat them up, yum!

Linguine with Clam Sauce

by Liz Ballo

The most remarkable thing about my mother is that for thirty years she served the family nothing but leftovers. The original meal has never been found.

Calvin Trillin

Ingredients

6 dozen littleneck clams,
  scrubbed under cold running water

Extra virgin olive oil

6 garlic cloves, peeled,
  but kept whole and smashed

1 cup white wine

½ cup water

1 large pinch crushed red pepper flakes

1 lb linguine

2 tbsps butter

2 tbsps parsley, chopped

1 cup grated parmesan

Kosher salt

Method

In a large sauté pan add a few tablespoons of olive oil and the garlic cloves. Bring the pan to a medium heat and cook until the garlic becomes golden. Add the 6 dozen clams to the pan with the wine, ½ cup of water and a good size pinch of the red pepper flakes. Cover the pan and bring it to a boil over medium heat until the clams open, about 10 minutes.

While the clams are cooking, bring a large pot of water to a boil over medium heat. Add a good pinch of salt. Drop the linguine into the salted boiling water and cook until the pasta is al dente, maybe a minute or so less than the package directs. Before you drain the cooked pasta, reserve 1 cup of the water it cooked in and put aside.

When the clams are cooked, remove them from the pan with a slotted spoon but continue to cook the remaining cooking liquid for an extra 1–2 minutes to reduce. Let the clams cool a bit, and then remove 4 dozen from their shells, reserving the clams but discarding the shells. Keep the remaining 2 dozen clams in their shells and cover with foil to keep warm. Pour the cooking liquid through a muslin cloth into a measuring cup.

Put the strained clam cooking liquid back into a clean large sauté pan and then add the butter and cooked clams that have been removed from their shells. Bring the liquid to a boil and toss in the cooked pasta and the herbs. Cook the pasta together with the sauce for a few minutes until the sauce clings to the pasta. If the sauce seems a bit dry, add a few tablespoons of the reserved pasta cooking water. When done, turn off the heat and toss in the grated parmesan, then finish with a drizzle of olive oil. Toss to combine.

Divide the pasta into serving dishes and garnish with the clams that are still in their shells and a little more shaved parmesan.

Tasty Lamb Burgers

by Pamela Thomas

Well, Clarice – have the lambs stopped screaming?
Hannibal Lecter, *The Silence of the Lambs*, Thomas Harris

Ingredients

1½ lbs minced lamb
  (it is best not to use lean mince as fat will help to bind the burgers and keep them moist)

1 small onion, finely chopped

2 cloves garlic, crushed

1 tsp cumin seeds, crushed

2 green chilies, medium heat, finely chopped

1 tbsp fresh mint, chopped

1 tsp coriander seeds, crushed

½ tsp black pepper

1 tsp salt

Method

Place the lamb in a large bowl and add the remaining ingredients. Mix it all altogether until just combined. This is best done by hand but don't overwork the mixture or the burger will be tough.

Wet your hands, then shape the mixture into 4–6 burgers.

The burgers can now be cooked either on a griddle pan or non-stick frying pan with a drop of oil. During the summer, these should definitely be cooked on the grill. Make sure you preheat the frying pan, griddle pan or grill to a medium heat. Cook the burgers for about 5 minutes on each side, turning them only once.

Serve with pita bread, salad and tzatziki dip (recipe on page 121).

Serves 4–6

Honey and Mustard Salmon with Butter Bean Mash

by Adrienne Truelove

*The Interior Department is in charge of salmon while they're in fresh water,
but the Commerce Department handles them when they're in salt water,
and I hear it gets even more complicated once they're smoked.*
President Obama, 2011 State of the Union Address

Ingredients

4 medium-size, skinless salmon fillets

1 lime

3 tbsps clear honey

1 tbsp whole-grain mustard

3 15 oz cans butter beans, rinsed

2 tbsps butter

5 tbsps crème fraîche

1 garlic clove, crushed

4 oz arugula or rocket salad (one large handful)

Method

Set the grill to its highest setting. Put the salmon fillets evenly spaced in a shallow flameproof dish. Finely grate the zest of the lime into a bowl, then squeeze in the juice and stir in the honey, mustard and a good sprinkling of salt. Pour the mixture over the salmon and grill, without turning, for 5–6 minutes until it's golden on top and cooked through (check the center with a fork).

Meanwhile, tip the beans into a saucepan and add the butter, crème fraîche, garlic and plenty of salt and pepper. Turn the heat to moderate and coarsely mash everything together – a wooden spoon or a masher will do the job – until hot and bubbling. This only takes a few minutes as the beans are already cooked. Tip in the rocket and stir into the mash until it's hot and just wilted.

Serve the salmon on the mash, drizzled with the cooking juices from the pan the salmon was cooked in.

Serves 4

Chili

by Chris Hill

Wish I had time for just one more bowl of chili.
Last words of Kit Carson, American frontiersman (1809–1868)

Ingredients

1½ lbs lean ground beef

8 oz smoked sausage, such as
  Andouille or Italian sausage

1 cup chopped onion

1 red or green bell pepper, chopped

2 cloves garlic, minced

1 can (4oz) mild green chili peppers

2–3 tbsps diced jalapeno peppers,
  or to taste

2 cans (14½ oz each)
  diced tomatoes, undrained

1 can (8oz) tomato sauce

1 can (15oz) black beans, drained and rinsed

1 tsp paprika

2–3 tbsps chili powder

½ tsp ground cumin

¼ tsp ground black pepper

1 tsp salt, or to taste

Method

Take sausage out of its casing and dice into ½-inch bites. In a large skillet brown the ground beef and sausage with onion until meat is no longer pink.

Add the bell pepper and garlic and cook, stirring, for about 1 minute longer.

Transfer to a slow cooker, or cast-iron or other heavy casserole dish, and combine remaining ingredients; cover and cook on LOW for 4–6 hours. If you're cooking it in a casserole in the oven you might find it cooks much quicker, so check after a few hours.

Serve with sour cream and grated cheddar.

Serves 6–8

Warm Shrimp and Lentil Salad

by Charlotte Santin

Ingredients

8 oz French green (de Puy) lentils,
 picked over and rinsed

2 large stalks celery, finely chopped

1 medium (6–8oz) onion,
 finely chopped

1 large carrot, finely chopped

4 cloves garlic, crushed

1 bay leaf

3 cups water

3 sprigs fresh thyme,
 plus additional for garnish

8 large shrimp, shelled and deveined,
 or you can leave shells on if you like

5 tbsps extra virgin olive oil

½ cup fresh flat-leaf parsley leaves,
 finely chopped

2 tbsps sherry vinegar

2 tsps Dijon mustard

1 red chili, deseeded and finely chopped

1 lime, juice and zest

Salt and pepper

Method

In 4-quart saucepan, combine lentils, celery, onion, carrot, half the garlic, bay leaf, water, and 3 thyme sprigs. Heat to boiling on medium-high. Reduce heat to medium-low; cover and simmer 25–35 minutes or until lentils are tender.

Meanwhile, while lentils simmer, place the shrimp in a shallow dish. Mix together the finely chopped chili, lime zest and juice, remaining garlic and 3 tablespoons of oil, then pour over the shrimp. Cover and chill for 20 minutes to marinate. Heat 12-inch grill pan on medium-high until very hot. Add shrimp in a single layer and cook 1–2 minutes or until browned. Turn shrimp over and cook 2 minutes longer or until shrimp just turn opaque throughout.

Drain lentil mixture well and transfer to large bowl. Remove and discard bay leaf and thyme sprigs. Toss lentil mixture with parsley, vinegar, mustard, remaining 2 tablespoons oil, salt and freshly ground black pepper. Divide salad among serving plates. Top each serving with 2 shrimp; garnish with thyme sprigs.

Chicken Piccata

by Grandma Derman

My grandmother is over eighty and still doesn't need glasses.
Drinks right out of the bottle.

Henny Youngman

Ingredients

4 (6oz) skinless, boneless chicken breast halves

¼ cup all-purpose flour

2 tbsps butter

1 tbsp olive oil

½ cup white wine

¼ cup fresh lemon juice

2 tbsps capers, rinsed and drained

2 tsps minced fresh garlic

¼ tsp salt

¼ tsp freshly ground black pepper

2 tbsps chopped fresh flat-leaf parsley

Method

Place each breast half between 2 sheets of heavy-duty plastic wrap; pound to ½-inch thickness using a meat mallet or small heavy skillet. Place flour, seasoned with salt and freshly ground black pepper, in a shallow dish, and dredge chicken in flour.

Heat butter and oil in a large skillet over medium-high heat. Add chicken, and cook for 3 minutes on each side or until browned. Remove chicken from pan; keep warm. Add white wine, lemon juice, capers, and garlic to pan; scrape pan to loosen browned bits. Cook for 2 minutes or until slightly thickened. Sprinkle with salt and pepper. Serve chicken over pasta. Top with sauce; sprinkle with parsley.

Serves 4

Slow Roasted Pulled Pork with Coleslaw

by Digger

Don't ever wrestle with a pig. You'll both get dirty, but the pig will enjoy it.
George Bernard Shaw

Ingredients

Dry rub:

3 tbsps paprika

1 tbsp garlic powder

1 tbsp brown sugar

1 tbsp dry mustard

3 tbsps coarse sea salt

5–7 lbs pork roast, preferably
   shoulder or Boston butt

Cider-vinegar
barbecue sauce:

1½ cups cider vinegar

1 cup yellow or brown mustard

½ cup ketchup

⅓ cup packed brown sugar

2 garlic cloves,
   peeled and smashed

1 tsp kosher salt

1 tsp cayenne pepper

½ tsp freshly ground
   black pepper

Pan drippings from the pork

12 hamburger buns
   or bulky rolls

Coleslaw, see Joyce and Kenny
   Clear's recipe (page 127)

Pickle spears, for garnish

Method

Mix the dry rub ingredients together in a small bowl. Pat the roast dry and rub the spice blend all over it. Cover and refrigerate for at least 1 hour, or up to overnight. Preheat the oven to 300°F. Put the pork in a roasting pan and roast it for about 6 hours. An instant-read thermometer stuck into the thickest part of the pork should register 170°F. Basically, you want to roast it until it's falling apart.

While the pork is roasting, make the barbecue sauce by combining the ingredients in a saucepan over medium heat. Simmer gently, stirring, for 10 minutes until the sugar dissolves. Take it off the heat and let it sit until you're ready to use it. After the roast is done, you can deglaze the pan with a cup of hot water and add the drippings to the barbecue sauce.

When the pork is done, take it out of the oven, put it onto a large platter. Allow the meat to rest for about 10 minutes. While the pork is still warm, you want to shred the meat using 2 forks. Using one to steady the meat, use the other to "pull" shreds of meat off the roast. Put the shredded pork in a bowl and pour most of the sauce over (hold a quarter of the sauce back to serve on the side). Stir it all up well so that the pork is coated with the sauce.

To serve, spoon the pulled pork mixture into each roll and top with some of Joyce and Kenny Clear's coleslaw (see page 127). This shredded pork is also great in taco shells!

Mussels in Curry Cream Sauce

by Joey Rees

Ingredients

½ cup minced shallots

2 tbsps minced garlic

1½ cups dry white wine

1 cup heavy (double) cream

1 tsp curry powder

32 mussels – cleaned and debearded

¼ cup butter

¼ cup minced parsley

¼ cup chopped green onions

Method

In a large saucepan, cook shallots and garlic in simmering wine until translucent. Stir in cream and curry powder. When sauce is heated through, add mussels. Cover, and steam mussels for a few minutes, until their shells open wide. With a slotted spoon, transfer steamed mussels to a bowl, leaving the sauce in the pan. Discard any unopened mussels.

Whisk butter into the cream sauce. Turn heat off, and stir in parsley and green onions. Pour over mussels and serve immediately.

Spicy Turkey Steaks with Mushroom Sauce

by Simon Fry

Ingredients

For the sauce:

2 dozen button mushrooms

Splash balsamic vinegar

2 tbsps unsalted butter

8 rashers bacon

2 bunches spring onions or scallions, cleaned and finely sliced

12 plum tomatoes diced into approx. ½-inch cubes

Fresh rosemary

For the turkey:

4 turkey steaks

2 red chilis, medium heat

2 green chilis, medium heat

2 inches ginger

1 lemon, zested

1 garlic bulb

Splash white wine

2 cups extra virgin olive oil

Freshly ground pepper

Sea salt

Method

For the marinade:

To make marinade, pour about ½-inch of olive oil into a large marinating dish. Remove stalks and deseed the red and green chilis. Peel a whole garlic bulb. Keep half and put half aside to use later. Trim and peel the ginger. Place all in a food blender or food processor and whizz up into a relatively fine mix. Add this to the marinating dish, season with a good pinch of sea salt, freshly ground black pepper, and the zest of about half of a lemon. Mix well.

Lay the turkey steaks on a chopping board and tenderize using a rolling pin. Avoid breaking the steaks as much as possible. Roll out the steaks to ¼ inch thickness and then add the flattened steaks to the marinating dish and place in the fridge for about 2 hours.

For the sauce:

Finely slice the remaining garlic cloves and, using a small frying pan with a good dollop of virgin olive oil, fry over a medium heat until dark golden, then transfer the garlic with a slotted spoon to some paper kitchen towels to remove any excess oil and put to one side.

Cut bacon horizontally into ½-inch strips, add to frying pan and cook until almost crispy. Move onto kitchen towel to remove any excess oil and put to one side.

Thoroughly wash the button mushrooms, add to same frying pan and cook with the butter on a medium heat for about 6–7 minutes, or until golden-brown. Add an extra splash of virgin olive oil if needed. Turn the heat up to full and add a generous dousing of balsamic vinegar. Keep the extractor fan going as this will tend to fume. Cook for about a minute or until the balsamic is at least 50 percent reduced. Tip the mushrooms into a bowl, cover the bowl and put to one side to steam and marinate.

Remove the leaves from 3 or 4 stalks of rosemary and finely chop. Add these to a clean frying pan with a splash of olive oil. Cook over medium heat until the chopped leaves begin to brown, add spring onions and turn the heat up. Cook for 3 or 4 minutes, then set aside.

Using the same pan, cook the tomatoes on high until they begin to break down and then add the zest of half a lemon into the mix. Turn into a covered dish to keep warm or place in a warming tray.

For the turkey:

Heat a clean deep frying pan on high, then add the turkey steaks. Ensure the pan is hot prior to adding the steaks and cook on a medium heat until golden on both sides. Add the marinade when the steaks are nearly done and turn the heat back up. Add the mushrooms and the onions and mix well with the steaks.

When everything is hot, turn out onto a large serving plate. Add the tomatoes in the center of the plate and sprinkle the garlic chips on the tomatoes.

Serve with lightly boiled broccoli or mange tout.

Serves 4 "normal" people or Simon plus one

Saffron and Lemon Chicken with Crispy Rice

by Margo Marrone

*The best way to execute French cooking is to get good and loaded
and whack the hell out of a chicken. Bon appétit.*

Julia Child

Ingredients

Basmati rice (1 cup per person and 1 extra)

½ cup butter (less if only 1 or 2 people)

4 chicken breasts, boneless, skinless
  and cut into 2-inch pieces

1 garlic clove, peeled and crushed

1 shallot, finely chopped

½ tsp saffron

1 tbsp olive oil

1 lemon, juiced

Salt

Method

Wash the rice in lukewarm water until it runs clear (this removes some of the starch that makes the rice sticky). Put the rice in a bowl and add enough cold water to cover the rice. Add ½ teaspoon of salt per cup of rice to water and leave it to soak for a minimum 1 hour in cold water or preferably overnight.

Put the chicken in a bowl; add the juice from the lemon, the crushed garlic, finely chopped shallot, olive oil and ½ teaspoon of saffron. Cover and let it marinate overnight or at least 1 hour.

Boil 2 quarts of water and add 2 tablespoons salt. Drain the rice and add it to the boiling water allowing it to boil for 10 minutes until al dente. Strain the rice and wash with cold water to prevent further cooking.

In a non-stick pan melt half the butter and add 2 tablespoons of water. Add the rice to the pan, spoon by spoon, making sure the bottom is evenly covered. Add all the rice until a mountain is formed. Put the rest of the butter on top and put on a low heat. Cover with a kitchen towel or cloth, then put the lid on and allow it to cook under a very low heat for 1 hour. This will prevent any water going back into the pot and the rice should come out fluffy and light with a beautiful golden crispy base.

Tip – to empty the rice, soak the bottom of the pan in cold water, then put a plate on top and flip it over like a tarte tatin. For an extra touch, take out 4 spoonfuls of rice and mix it with a pinch of saffron and add it back to the rice. This will give it a lovely color.

Put the chicken on skewers, season with salt and, if possible, barbeque. If you don't have a barbeque then cook on a griddle pan until golden.

When the chicken is done, serve on top of the rice. This is great served with a finely chopped tomato, cucumber, coriander and mint salad.

Grilled Mako Shark Tacos with Tangy Texas Slaw

by Philip Aviles

Every summer Oak Bluffs at Martha's Vineyard hosts a big-game fishing competition called the Annual Monster Shark Tournament. This is a great time to make this recipe. However, you can also use swordfish or halibut or any firm white fish.

Ingredients

For tacos:

2 lb Mako shark fillet,
  ½-inch thick and skinless

½ tsp chopped parsley

½ tsp chopped cilantro (coriander)

2 tbsps extra virgin olive oil

½ tsp ancho chile powder or
  mild chili powder (not cayenne)

¼ tsp ground black pepper

¼ tsp kosher salt

Juice of 1 lime

8 fresh corn tortillas (Mexican-style)

8 lime wedges for garnish

For coleslaw:

½ head of cabbage, sliced finely
  (a napa or Chinese cabbage is best)

1 jalapeno pepper sliced finely

1 small onion, sliced finely

1 tbsp chopped cilantro (coriander)

1 tbsp mayonnaise

1 tbsp sour cream

½ tbsp mustard

½ tsp kosher salt

¼ tsp ground white pepper

Juice of 1 lemon

Method

To prepare coleslaw:

Combine all coleslaw ingredients in large bowl and mix. Refrigerate for at least 1 hour before preparing fish tacos, stirring occasionally.

To prepare tacos:

Cut the fillet into 16 3-inch strips. Place them in a bowl with the rest of the taco ingredients and marinate for at least ½ hour. Put grill on medium-high and oil grill with vegetable oil. Grill fish for about 2 minutes on each side; it should be firm to touch but not hard. When the fish is cooked, reserve it in a warm spot. While the grill is still hot, grill tortillas for 30 seconds on each side. Then place 2 tortillas per person on each plate. Add 1 tablespoon of coleslaw per taco then 2 strips of grilled fish. Garnish with lime wedges. Serve with guacamole on the side (see page 159 for recipe).

Serves 4

Kofta Kebabs with Fresh Tabbouleh Salad

by Noor

Ingredients

For koftas:

2 lb minced lamb

2 onions, finely grated

6 garlic cloves, peeled and crushed

2 tsps dried chili flakes

1 small bunch of flat-leaf parsley, chopped

2 tsps ground cumin

3 tsps tumeric

1 tsp cinnamon

Olive oil

Sea salt and freshly ground black pepper

For tabbouleh:

½ cup fine bulgur wheat

3 tbsps olive oil

2 cups fresh flat-leaf parsley, finely chopped

½ cup fresh mint, finely chopped

2 medium tomatoes, cut into ¼-inch pieces

½ cucumber, peeled, deseeded, and cut into ¼-inch pieces

3 tbsps fresh lemon juice

¾ tsp salt

¼ tsp black pepper

Method

To make the tabbouleh:

Stir together bulgur and 1 tablespoon of oil in a bowl. Pour 1 cup of boiling-hot water over the mixture, then cover bowl tightly with plastic wrap and let stand 15 minutes.

Drain in a sieve, pressing on bulgur to remove any excess liquid.

Transfer bulgur to a bowl and toss with remaining ingredients, including 2 tablespoons oil, until well combined.

To make the koftas:

Preheat a charcoal barbecue or grill 40 minutes ahead of cooking, or a gas barbecue or grill 10 minutes ahead of cooking. If using a cast-iron griddle pan, heat it over a high heat, then lower the heat slightly before cooking.

Put the minced lamb into a bowl with the onions, garlic, chili flakes, parsley, spices, 1 teaspoon of salt and some freshly ground black pepper. Mix together with your hands until bound together.

Divide the mixture into 8 and mould it into long sausage shapes around skewers.

Brush the kofta generously with oil and lightly oil the bars of the barbecue, grill or griddle. Cook for 5 minutes, turning occasionally, until browned all over and cooked through. Serve with the tabbouleh and warm pitas.

Side Bites

Boston Baked Beans

by Mike Ballo

It's the molasses in this recipe that links it to Boston. In colonial times when the city was a trade center for rum from the Caribbean, molasses was a vital ingredient in rum production. The Boston Molasses Disaster of 1919 saw a huge tank of molasses explode, flooding the streets of the North End in sticky goo. You can still pick up the sweet scent on a hot summer's day.

Although traditionally cooked in an oven, Boston baked beans lend themselves perfectly to slow cookers, which is the method I use here.

Ingredients

1 lb (2–2¼ cups) dry white beans such as Navy beans or Great Northern beans (can also use kidney beans)

⅓ cup molasses

⅓ cup brown sugar

4 tbsps Dijon mustard

⅛ tsp ground cloves

3 cups hot water

½ lb salt pork (you can substitute bacon), cut into ½–1-inch pieces

1 medium onion (1½ cups), chopped

Method

Place beans in a large pot and cover with 2 inches of water. Soak overnight and drain. Alternatively, bring a pot with the beans covered with 2 inches of water to a boil, remove from heat and let soak for an hour, then drain.

Mix the molasses, brown sugar, mustard, and ground cloves with 3 cups of hot water.

Line the bottom of a slow cooker (or a Dutch oven if you are cooking in the oven) with half of the salt pork. Layer over with half of the drained beans. Add all of the onions in a layer, and then top with another layer of beans and the remaining salt pork. Pour the molasses and water mixture over the beans to just cover the beans.

Cover and cook in a slow cooker on the low setting for 8 hours or in a 250°F oven, until the beans are tender. If you're cooking in the oven instead of a slow cooker, your beans will probably take less time to cook. Check after a few hours to see if the beans are tender. Also, check the water level a few hours in, and if the beans need more water (which they probably will), add some. Add additional salt to taste if needed. Best the next day.

Cornbread

by Katie Bartlett

You will NEVER taste cornbread moister than this. Many have sneered at its unauthentic ingredients. However, even the most tiresome critics have been silenced – and you know who you are.

Ingredients

2 small cans diced green chilies
  (or a couple tbsps of chopped jalapenos from a jar)

1 can creamed-style corn

1 box corn muffin mix

1 large onion, grated

2 cups grated cheddar cheese
  (I use one with a little jalapeno or habanero for a little extra kick)

3 eggs, beaten

½ cup milk

½ cup vegetable oil

Method

Preheat oven to 375˚F. Mix all ingredients together and pour into a 9 x 13-inch cake pan. Bake for 1 hour. Check to see if a toothpick inserted into the middle comes out clean; if it does, it's done.

Cut into squares.

Tzatziki Dip

by Suzo Wallace

Hey yogurt, if you're so cultured, how come I never see you at the opera?
Attributed to Stephen Colbert

This Greek sauce is a great accompaniment to any grilled meat or fish, especially lamb. I enjoy it in a hot pita with salad and a kebab. I've listed the amounts of the ingredients I use, but that's more of a guideline. Taste it as you go along – especially when adding the garlic and herbs. It's very important to deseed the cucumber and drain it of its water as much as possible before mixing it with the other ingredients. It makes all the difference.

Ingredients

One medium-size cucumber

3 tbsps extra virgin olive oil

2 cups Greek yogurt, strained
  (you can substitute strained plain yogurt)

2 garlic cloves, peeled and crushed

2 tbsps fresh mint or dill, chopped

½ lemon, juiced

Spring onions (scallions), finely chopped

A little salt

Method

Peel a cucumber, cut it in half and remove the seeds. Finely chop or grate it and leave it in a colander with a little salt until it has given up most of its juice. Pat the cucumber dry with kitchen towels and then fold into olive oil and 2 cups of strained yogurt. Season with crushed cloves of garlic and mint or dill, a squeeze of lemon juice and spring onions. The spring onions are optional; taste it before you add them.

Make this an hour before serving so the flavors blend.

Caesar Salad

by Happy Butterworth Bartlett

According to legend, on July 4th, 1924, the salad was created on a busy weekend at Caesar Cardini's Restaurant in Tijuana, Mexico. It is said that Caesar was short of supplies and didn't want to disappoint the customers so he concocted this salad with what was on hand. To add flair to this he prepared it at the table. The Caesar soon became a hit and celebrities such as Clark Gable, W.C. Fields, Wallis Simpson and Julia Childs travelled to the Mexican restaurant just to get the salad.

Ingredients

1 onion, quartered

2 oz flat anchovy fillets

2 cloves of garlic, peeled

1 quart (2 pints) vegetable oil

2 tbsps lemon juice

¼ cup of water

3 tbsps cider vinegar

⅓ tsp white pepper

2 tsps salt

⅓ tsp dry mustard

6 eggs, room temperature

Romaine lettuce

Croutons (see Julia Sullivan's gazpacho recipe on page 51 for homemade)

Parmesan cheese, grated

Method

Mince together onion, anchovies and garlic in a food processor. While blending, add the lemon juice, water, vinegar, salt, pepper, mustard and eggs one at a time. Blend for a total of 4–5 minutes, while slowly drizzling in the oil in a steady stream, taking care not to add too quickly, otherwise it could separate.

Chill and serve over romaine lettuce. Sprinkle with homemade croutons and freshly grated parmesan cheese and toss.

Coleslaw

by Joyce and Kenny Clear

Here's the thing about coleslaw. The muck you get at restaurants or grocery stores is disgusting. It was probably made in a vat (the size of a football field), in the Midwest somewhere at the turn of the century and has somehow ended up on your plate. Fresh, homemade slaw is easy to make and tastes awesome!

Ingredients

½ head of white cabbage

½ head of red cabbage

1 medium-size Vidalia or other sweet onion

3 small carrots

1½ cups mayonnaise

3 tbsps white wine vinegar

¾ cup water

1 tbsp sugar

Salt and pepper to taste

Method

Slice the cabbage, carrots and onion as thin as possible using a mandoline.

In a bowl, whisk the mayonnaise, vinegar, water, and sugar. Combine with cabbage, onion and carrots. Mix well and let sit overnight. (Keep mixing so everything soaks in the sauce.)

Add salt and pepper to taste.

Hash in a Hurry

by Mickey Cobb

He took the Who's feast, he took the Who pudding, he took the roast beast.
He cleaned out that ice box as quick as a flash.
Why, the Grinch even took their last can of Who hash.

How the Grinch Stole Christmas, Dr. Seuss

Ingredients

4 tbsps butter

1 cup chopped onion

2 cups chopped cooked corned beef
 (you can also use leftover roast beef)

1½ cups small diced cooked beets

1½ cups small diced cooked potato

1 tsp Worcestershire sauce

¼ cup fresh parsley, chopped

Freshly ground black pepper to taste

Method

Heat butter in a frying pan on medium-high heat. It's best to use a cast-iron pan so the hash gets a nice brown crust. Add the onions and cook for a couple of minutes, until translucent.

Add the corned beef, potatoes, and beets. Stir in the pan to combine, and spread out evenly in the pan. Reduce the heat to medium. Press down with a metal spatula to help brown the mixture. Don't stir, but just let cook until nicely browned on one side, then use a metal spatula to lift up sections of the mixture and turn over to brown the other side. If the mixture sticks to the pan too much, just add a little more butter to the pan where it's sticking.

When nicely browned, remove from heat. Sprinkle in some Worcestershire sauce. Stir in freshly chopped parsley and freshly ground black pepper to taste. There should be enough salt from the corned beef, but if not, add salt to taste.

Serve plain or with fried or poached eggs on top.

Serves 4

Sweet Bites

Key Lime Pie

by Lisa F. Baker

Key limes were named after the Florida Keys. Key lime pie became popular in the 1950s – a custard-like pie made with lime juice, condensed milk, and eggs and served in a pastry shell. Key limes are yellow and rather bitter, unlike Lisa who faithfully makes Mike this pie EVERY summer.

Ingredients

For the crust:

16 graham crackers, crushed

3 tbsps sugar

¼ lb margarine or butter, melted

For the pie:

4 large or extra large egg yolks

1 14 oz can sweetened condensed milk

½ cup fresh key lime juice
(approximately 30 key limes or… I hate to admit this… 4 or 5 regular limes – tastes the same)

2 tsps grated lime peel

Whipping cream for garnish (optional)

½ cup whipping cream

2 tsps granulated sugar

¼ tsp vanilla

Method

For the crust:

Mix the ingredients and press them into a 9-inch pie plate. Bake in a preheated 350°F oven for 10–12 minutes until lightly browned. Place on a rack to cool.

For the pie filling:

Use an electric mixer and beat the egg yolks until they are thick and turn to a light yellow – don't overmix. Turn the mixer off and add the sweetened condensed milk. Turn speed to low and mix in half of the lime juice. Once the juice is incorporated, add the other half of the juice and the zest, continue to mix until blended (just a few seconds). Pour the mixture into the pie shell and bake at 350°F for 12 minutes to set the yolks and kill any salmonella in the eggs.

Just before you serve, whip up cream, sugar and vanilla and spread over cooled pie.

Chocolate Bundt Cake

by Chatham Moss

No other factory in the world mixes its chocolate by waterfall.
But it's the only way if you want it just right.
Charlie and the Chocolate Factory, Roald Dahl

This dark chocolate Bundt cake is a chocolate lover's dream. This is a delicious and intensely chocolate cake. If you really want to make it special use a good-quality Dutch cocoa.

Ingredients

8 oz butter (2 sticks)

½ cup Dutch process cocoa,
  or any high-quality chocolate cocoa

¾ cup water

2 cups granulated sugar

1 cup sour cream

1 tbsp vanilla extract

2 large eggs

2 cups all-purpose flour, stir before measuring

1 tsp baking soda (add ½ tsp
  more if using standard baking cocoa)

½ tsp salt

For the dark chocolate glaze:

4 oz bittersweet chocolate

⅓ cup heavy (double) whipping cream

¼ cup light corn syrup
  (or golden syrup)

1 tsp vanilla extract

Method

Grease and flour a 10–12 cup Bundt pan. Heat oven to 350°F.

Melt butter in a large saucepan over medium-low heat; add cocoa, stirring until smooth. Whisk in the water and remove from heat. To the warm cocoa mixture, add the sugar, sour cream, 1 tablespoon vanilla, and eggs; whisk until smooth. In another bowl combine the flour, soda, and salt. Add all at once to the first mixture, whisking until well blended.

Pour batter into prepared pan. Bake for 35–40 minutes, or until it feels firm to the touch and has slightly pulled away from the sides of the pan. Cool in pan on a rack for 20 minutes. Carefully loosen the cake with a knife and invert onto a large plate. If using a pan with ridges, it should come out fine if properly greased and floured, without the need to loosen with a knife.

Meanwhile, prepare the glaze.

Chop chocolate and put in a small bowl; set aside. Combine the remaining heavy (double) whipping cream, corn syrup, and 1 teaspoon vanilla extract in a small saucepan. Cook the mixture, stirring, until it boils. Pour over the chocolate and whisk until smooth. Let cool to room temperature then spoon over the cooled cake. If too thick, thin with a little more cream.

Garnish with chopped walnuts.

Serves 10–12

Almond and Poppy Seed Bread

by Wendy "Mimi" Buffington

Ingredients (for 2 loaves)

3 eggs, slightly beaten

2¼ cups granulated sugar

1⅓ cups vegetable oil

1½ cups of milk

2 cups of flour

1½ tsps baking powder

1½ tsps salt

3 tbsps poppy seeds

2 tsps almond extract

For the glaze:

¼ cup frozen orange juice, thawed

¾ cup powdered sugar

½ tsp vanilla

1 tsp almond extract

Method

Grease and flour 2 loaf pans. Beat together eggs, sugar, oil, and milk. Separately, combine baking powder, flour and salt and then beat into egg mixture. Stir in poppy seeds, almond extract and pour into loaf pans.

Bake at 350˚F for 50–60 minutes.

To make the glaze, combine ingredients. Let breads cool in pans for 10 minutes.
Remove breads from the pans and then spread the glaze over the tops while still warm.

Boston Cream Pie

by Father Anthony

Ingredients

For the cake:

6 tbsps butter, softened

2 tbsps all-purpose flour

1½ cups cake flour (to make cake flour, put 1½ cups of regular all-purpose flour in a bowl, remove 3 tbsps of flour and replace with cornstarch – sift well)

2 tsps baking powder

¼ tsp salt

¾ cup white sugar

2 eggs

1 tsp vanilla extract

½ cup milk

For the custard:

½ cup light (single) cream

½ cup milk

¼ cup white sugar

1 pinch salt

4 tsps cornstarch (cornflour)

2 eggs

½ tsp vanilla extract

For the chocolate sauce:

2 tbsps butter

¼ cup light (single) cream

½ tsp vanilla extract

½ cup confectioners' sugar

3 oz semisweet chocolate, chopped

Method

Preheat oven to 375°F. Grease and flour 2 9-inch round cake pans. Sift the all-purpose flour, cake flour, baking powder and salt together and set aside. In a deep bowl, cream 6 tablespoons of the butter with ¾ cup sugar until light and fluffy. Beat in the 2 eggs, one at a time, then beat in the vanilla extract. Add the flour mixture alternately with the ½ cup of the milk in 3 stages, beating the batter smooth after each new stage is added. Divide the batter between the 2 prepared pans. Bake at 375°F for 15 minutes or until cakes begin to shrink away from the sides of the pans and the centers spring back when lightly touched. Turn the cakes onto wire racks to cool.

To make the custard:

Combine the ½ cup light (single) cream with ¼ cup of the milk and cook over medium heat until bubbles begin to form around the edge of the pan. Immediately add ¼ cup of the sugar and the salt, stirring until dissolved. Remove the pan from the heat. In a small bowl, combine ¼ cup of the milk with the cornstarch and whisk to remove lumps. Whisk in the 2 eggs. Add the hot cream mixture in a thin stream, whisking constantly. Return the mixture to the saucepan, bring to a boil and cook over low heat, stirring constantly, until the custard thickens and is smooth (about 5 minutes). Remove from heat and stir in ½ teaspoon vanilla and allow to cool to room temperature.

To make the chocolate sauce:

In a heavy saucepan over low heat, stir the chocolate pieces and 2 tablespoons butter until they are completely melted. Remove from the heat and, stirring constantly, add the ¼ cup light (single) cream in a thin steady stream. When mixture is smooth, stir in the confectioners' sugar and beat vigorously. Stir in ½ teaspoon vanilla.

To assemble cake, spread the cooled filling over one of the cooled cakes and place the second cake on top. Pour the chocolate frosting evenly over the top, allowing it to spill down the sides.

Blueberry Pie

by Ciara Parkes

Sticky, spicy and full of fruit. Well, it's Ciara's pie.

You ought to have seen what I saw on my way
To the village, through Mortenson's pasture to-day:
Blueberries as big as the end of your thumb,
Real sky-blue, and heavy, and ready to drum
In the cavernous pail of the first one to come!
And all ripe together, not some of them green
And some of them ripe! You ought to have seen!

"Blueberries", Robert Frost

Ingredients

¾ cup sugar

2½ tbsps cornstarch (cornflour)

¼ tsp salt

¼ tsp cinnamon

⅔ cup water

5 cups fresh blueberries

1 tsp vanilla extract

2 tbsps butter

2 tsps freshly squeezed lemon juice

1 tsp finely grated lemon zest
(yellow only, not white part)

10-inch pie crust, blind-baked and cooled

Method

If you want to use ready-made pie crust, feel free! Why exhaust yourself making pie dough?!
It is summer, after all. However, you should use fresh blueberries and REAL butter.

In a medium saucepan, combine sugar, cornstarch, salt and cinnamon. Blend in water and
1½ cups blueberries. Bring to a boil and smash half the berries (a wooden spoon or an old-
fashion potato masher does the trick). Continue to stir constantly until mixture is very thick, a
minute or so. Remove from heat and stir in vanilla extract, butter, lemon juice and lemon zest.
You must let this cool before proceeding. If you're in a hurry, you can cool the filling quicker
by submerging the bottom of the pan in a bowl of ice and water while stirring.

Fold in 2½ cups blueberries, coating them well. Scoop into a cooled baked pie shell.
Arrange remaining cup of fresh berries over top. Cover with plastic wrap and chill at least
2 hours, or overnight if possible.

To serve, remove pie from refrigerator and allow it to come to room temperature. Serve with
whipped cream or vanilla ice cream

Serves 8

Sticky Toffee Pudding

by Charlie Pillsbury

Sticky Toffee Pudding has to be made with dates. However a lot of people don't like them. That's why we like this recipe – because the dates are puréed so you get a hint of flavor without the texture. This is the best dessert in the world. However, don't take my word for that. As we Englishmen, like to say, "The proof of the pudding is in the eating."

Ingredients

2 oz butter, plus extra for greasing

6 oz demerara sugar

1 tbsp golden syrup (corn syrup)

2 free-range eggs

2 tbsps black treacle (molasses)

7 oz self-raising flour,
   plus extra for flouring

7 oz pitted dates

10 fl oz boiling water

1 tsp baking soda

½ tsp vanilla extract

For the sauce:

4 fl oz heavy (double) cream

2 oz butter, diced

2 oz dark muscovado sugar

2 tbsps black treacle (molasses)

1 tbsp golden syrup (corn syrup)

Vanilla ice cream, to serve

Method

Preheat the oven to 400°F. Grease and flour 6 7 oz individual pudding molds or ramekins.

Cream the butter and sugar together in a food processor or with a hand mixer until pale and fluffy. Add the golden syrup, treacle and eggs, a little at a time, and blend until smooth. Add the flour and blend, at a low speed, until well combined.

Meanwhile, blend the dates and boiling water in a food processor to a smooth purée. Stir in the baking soda and vanilla. Pour the date mixture into the pudding batter and stir until well combined. Pour the mixture into the molds and bake for 20–25 minutes, or until the top is springy and golden-brown.

To make the sauce, heat all of the ingredients in a pan, stirring occasionally, until boiling.

To serve, remove the puddings from the molds and place onto 6 serving plates.
Pour over the sauce and serve with a scoop of vanilla ice cream.

Serves 6

Delectable Chocolate Brownies

by Shamim Sarif

Every day Hanan gives Shamim a list of things to do. Every day Shamim puts "eat chocolate" at the top of that list so she's sure to get at least one thing done.

Ingredients

6 oz dark chocolate (70% cocoa)

6 oz butter

9 oz superfine (caster) sugar

3 eggs

1 tsp vanilla extract

3 oz flour

Method

Melt the chocolate and butter together in a bowl placed over a pan of simmering water (the bowl shouldn't be touching the water). Or you can use the shortcut that I inevitably use, and put the bowl in the microwave – it has to be at a low heat – for a few minutes.

In a separate bowl, whisk the eggs and sugar together well, until the mixture is light and thick.

Add the vanilla extract to the egg mixture. Try to use extract rather than essence – it costs a lot more, but there is a big difference in taste. Then pour in the warm chocolate and mix gently but thoroughly into the egg and sugar mixture.

Fold in the flour. If you like nuts in your brownies, this is the time to throw in a handful of pecans, walnuts, or whatever you like best. However, I believe nuts just take up space where chocolate ought to be.

Preheat oven to 300°F and butter a square tin, about 8 x 8 inches.

Bake brownies for about 25 minutes. The key is to cook it just enough so that the edges are shrinking slightly away from the sides but so that it is still quite soft to the touch or even slightly wobbly in the middle.

That will give the brownie the fudge center rather than make it into a moist cake.

Let it cool, cut into squares and serve with a big scoop of ice cream, chocolate syrup and fruit!

Strawberry and Cinnamon Cake

by Mark Creedy Smith

Strawberries that in gardens grow
Are plump and juicy fine,
But sweeter far as wise men know
Spring from the woodland vine.

"Wild Strawberries", Robert Graves

Ingredients

¾ cup ground almonds

¾ cup butter, softened

¾ cup golden superfine (caster) sugar

¾ cup self-raising flour

1 tsp ground cinnamon

1 large egg, plus 1 egg yolk

2 cups strawberries, hulled and sliced

Confectioner's sugar, for dusting

Whipped heavy (double) cream mixed with
  Greek yogurt (half and half is good), to serve

Method

Preheat the oven to 350°F. Line the bottom of a 9-inch springform pan with greaseproof paper and butter the sides.

Mix almonds, butter, sugar, flour, cinnamon, egg and egg yolk in a food processor just until the ingredients are evenly combined. Spread half the mixture over the base of the pan in a smooth layer with no gaps – easiest to do this with two forks. Lay the sliced strawberries on top.
Add the remaining cake mixture and spread it as best you can, but don't worry if a few strawberries peep through.

Bake for 1 hour (it may need an extra 5 minutes), but check after 40 minutes – if it is getting too brown, cover loosely with foil. The cake should be slightly risen and dark golden-brown when cooked.

Cool in the pan slightly, then loosen the edges with a knife and remove from the pan. Slide the cake onto a plate and sprinkle with a dusting of icing sugar. Serve warm or cold, in wedges with dollops of cream and Greek yogurt.

Apple Pie

by Aunt Francie

On the Stroud family apple farm, everyone learned how to make apple pie, but no one made it better than Aunt Francie. She was always kind, funny and wonderful with kids. This was her "secret" recipe.

Ingredients

2 cups sifted all-purpose flour

½ tsp salt

⅔ cup vegetable shortening

4–5 tbsps of cold water

5–8 Granny Smith apples (green)

⅔ cup sugar

1 tbsp flour

1 tsp cinnamon

¼ tsp nutmeg

2 tbsps margarine or butter

2 tbsps of milk

½ lemon

Method

To make the pastry, combine flour, salt and vegetable shortening. Make a well in the middle of the mixture and add water. Mix and roll dough into two balls. Chill for 30 minutes.

Meanwhile, mix sugar, 1 tablespoon of flour, cinnamon and nutmeg in a bowl. Peel, and slice the apples into another small bowl.

Preheat oven to 400°F.

Roll out one of the balls and use it to line the bottom of a pie plate. Spread half of the sugar mix on top of bottom crust. Spread the sliced apples on top of that. Squeeze the juice of half a lemon on top of apples and then top with remaining sugar mixture.

Roll out the second ball of dough and top the pie. Wet the edges of the bottom crust with water to help the two crusts stick together then crimp the edges. With a small knife slice a few small slits into the top crust to let the steam out while it's cooking. Put milk into a small bowl and using a pastry brush paint the top of the pie. Sprinkle the top with a little sugar.

Bake at 400°F for 10 minutes, then 350°F for 40 minutes. When juice bubbles, test with a fork to see if the apples are tender. If it's getting too brown on top, cover with foil.

Serve with vanilla ice cream and enjoy.

Puffy French Toast with Strawberries and Cream

by Reno and Jan Antonietti

Ingredients

2 eggs

1 cup flour

1½ tsps baking powder

½ tsp salt

1 cup milk

8 slices whole wheat bread or leftover rolls,
  cut in half, firm is best

Vegetable oil

½ pint heavy (double) cream

2 cups fresh strawberries, sliced

1 cup fresh blueberries

Maple syrup (the real stuff)

Method

Preheat oven to 350°F.

Beat eggs and combine with baking powder, salt, flour and milk until smooth. Heat about 3 tablespoons of cooking oil in a deep frying pan over medium-high heat. Dip bread in egg mixture, flipping to soak both sides. Remix batter occasionally so the flour doesn't sink to the bottom. Place coated bread immediately into the hot pan and fry until golden-brown on both sides. This should only take 1–2 minutes; do not overcook. When done, remove the fried bread from the pan and drain on a paper towel. Then place in an ungreased baking dish and bake in a 350°F oven for about 10 minutes.

Whip heavy (double) cream until firm. Serve French toast warm with sliced strawberries, blueberries, whipped cream and warm maple syrup.

Serves 4

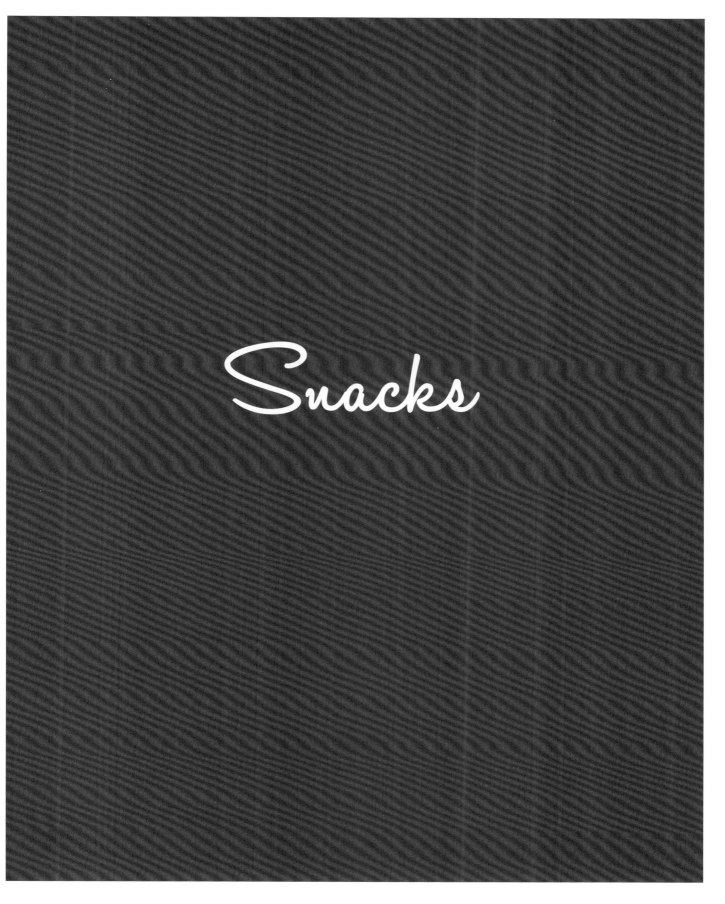

Snacks

Guacamole

4 Haas avocados

1–2 tsps kosher salt

½ tsp ground cumin

½ tsp cayenne

(If you don't have ground cumin or cayenne you can just add a few dashes of Tabasco)

½ red onion finely chopped

½ cup cilantro (coriander) finely chopped

1 clove garlic finely diced

½ lime juiced

1 tomato, deseeded and chopped

Cut avocados in half and discard pit. Using knife, score avocado, then scoop out. Roughly mash with fork and add all remaining ingredients. Cover with plastic wrap and let sit for 1 hour at room temperature.

Mom's Cheesy Squares

1 onion, finely chopped

1 ball of mozzarella, finely chopped

1 cup mayonnaise

1 loaf pumpernickel bread

Mix all the onion, mozzarella and mayonnaise together. Slice pumpernickel then cut each slice into 4 squares. Plop a dollop of the mixture onto each square and then put under broiler until golden-brown. It should only take a few minutes.

Blue Cheese Dressing

¾ cup of sour cream

½ tsp dry mustard

½ tsp black pepper

½ tsp salt

⅓ tsp garlic powder

1 tsp Worcestershire sauce

1⅓ cup mayonnaise

4 oz blue cheese (I prefer Danish Blue but Stilton, Gorgonzola or Roquefort will do)

In a mixing bowl combine sour cream, mustard, garlic powder, Worcestershire sauce, salt and pepper and stir for a few minutes. Add the mayonnaise and stir a few more minutes. Crumble the cheese into small pieces and add to mixture. Stir until mixed well. Let sit for 24 hours before using. Best served over iceberg lettuce with a sprinkle of crispy bacon bits.

Hot Artichoke Dip

10 oz frozen chopped spinach

2 14 oz cans artichoke hearts

½ cup mayonnaise

½ cup sour cream

1 cup freshly grated parmesan cheese

Preheat oven to 350°F. Defrost spinach in microwave then squeeze dry. Drain artichoke hearts and chop. Combine ingredients in bowl, then put in casserole dish and bake for 30 minutes until golden and bubbly.

Serve with crackers or bagel chips.

Roasted Corn Salsa

4 cups sweet yellow corn, shaved off the cob

½ red onion, diced

2 vine-ripened tomatoes, diced

2 tbsps cilantro (coriander), chopped

1 lime, juiced

1 jalapeno, deseeded and chopped

2 scallions, chopped

2 garlic cloves, diced

Few dashes of Tabasco

Kosher salt and pepper to taste

Over a large bowl shave kernels off cobs with a large knife until you have roughly 4 cups of corn. Heat non-stick skillet (no oil, this is dry roasted!) and cook corn kernels over medium to high heat for 10 minutes before turning them and cooking another 5 minutes. When the corn has a bit of color, add to a bowl with the rest of ingredients and mix together well. If possible, let it sit for a few hours so flavors can marry.

Serve with tortilla chips.

Cranberry Orange Chutney

12 oz fresh cranberries

1 cup water

¾ cup white sugar

½ cup orange juice

½ jalapeno pepper,
  deseeded and finely chopped

1 tsp cinnamon

¼ tsp ground allspice

2 tbsps zest of orange

In a medium saucepan, combine water and sugar and bring to a boil. Add cranberries and the rest of the ingredients. Bring to a boil again, then simmer for 10 minutes stirring often. Pour mixture into bowl, cover and refrigerate.

I love this chutney spread over cream cheese with wasabi rice crackers.

Chocolate Chippers

2½ cups flour

1 tsp baking soda

½ tsp salt

¼–⅓ cup Brewers yeast buds

¾ cup granulated sugar

¼ cup dark brown sugar

½ cup light brown sugar

1 tsp vanilla

1 cup softened butter

1 egg

12 oz chocolate chips

1 cup chopped walnuts or pecans

Preheat oven to 375°F.

Whisk the flour, baking soda, salt and yeast together in a small bowl.

Beat the granulated sugar, dark brown sugar, light brown sugar, vanilla and butter in a large mixer until smooth. Add the egg and mix well. Gradually add the dry ingredients and keep mixing. If it's too dry, add a bit of milk. Stir in chocolate chips and chopped walnuts.

Drop by tablespoons onto ungreased cookie sheets and back for 9–11 minutes.

Extras

How to Cook a Lobster

In order to boil your lobster, you will need a large pot with a lid.

Pour enough water in the pot to cover the lobster completely.

Add 2 tablespoons of sea salt for every 4 pints of water.

Bring the water to a fierce boil.

Grasp the live lobster behind the claws and drop it head first into the boiling water.

Cover the pot and once the water has started to boil again, start timing.

Boil the lobster for 10 minutes for the first pound of weight and then 3 more minutes for each extra pound. A 2 lb lobster will be done in 13 minutes, a 3 lb lobster in 16 minutes.

Once cooked, drain the lobster immediately (very important so lobster meat doesn't get mushy) and either serve hot or let cool.

How to Cook Steamers

This dish is commonly prepared with a kind of shellfish called steamers, a somewhat generic name that usually refers to a small soft-shell clam harvested from the sand banks and shallow waters along the coast of New England.

Hard shell clams, sometimes known as quahogs, can also be steamed. They are categorized by size – the smaller ones are called littlenecks, medium-size ones topnecks, and the larger ones cherrystones.

The New England clambake is a traditional preparation that includes clams layered with other ingredients such as corn, lobster, mussels, crabs, potatoes, and onions in a large metal bucket or drum. The layers are separated by seaweed and steamed over an outdoor fire.

Steamers usually come 12–15 per pound and you should estimate 1–2 pounds per person, depending on whether you're serving them as an appetizer or main course.

Ingredients

4 dozen clams

1 can of beer (not dark)

1 large onion, peeled and quartered

4 garlic cloves, crushed

1 linguica or chorizo sausage or hotdog

1 stick (4oz) of melted butter

Method

Buy fresh live clams. The shells should be closed and not broken. If a shell is open, tap on it lightly and it should close. If it doesn't, that usually means it's dead and you should throw it away.

Scrub the clams with a vegetable brush under cold water and then let them soak for an hour in a bucket of water. Adding a little coarse sea salt to the water will help remove the sand from the shells.

In a large stockpot, put beer, garlic, onion, linguica, and clams. It may not seem like enough liquid but don't worry; the clams will release a lot of water when cooking. Cover with a lid and bring to a slow boil over medium-high heat. Steam clams for 5–7 minutes or until all the clams are opened.

Transfer the cooked clams (if any are unopened, throw them away) into a large bowl using a slotted spoon, then strain the cooking broth through a muslin and put aside to keep warm.

To eat, remove the clam from its shell, then remove the black skin from its neck; wash the clam in the strained broth, dip it in the melted butter and pop it in your mouth!

Conversion Tables

Liquid or volume measures (approximate)

1 teaspoon		⅓ tablespoon	5ml/5cc
1 tablespoon	½ fluid ounce	3 teaspoons	15ml/15cc
2 tablespoons	1 fluid ounce	⅛ cup, 6 teaspoons	30ml/30cc
¼ cup	2 fluid ounces	4 tablespoons	59ml
⅓ cup	2⅔ fluid ounces	5 tablespoons + 1 teaspoon	79ml
½ cup	4 fluid ounces	8 tablespoons	118ml
⅔ cup	5⅓ fluid ounces	10 tablespoons + 2 teaspoons	158ml
¾ cup	6 fluid ounces	12 tablespoons	177ml
⅞ cup	7 fluid ounces	14 tablespoons	207ml
1 cup	8 fluid ounces/½ pint	16 tablespoons	237ml
2 cups	16 fluid ounces/1 pint	32 tablespoons	473ml
4 cups	32 fluid ounces	1 quart	946ml
1 pint	16 fluid ounces/1 pint	32 tablespoons	473ml
2 pints	32 fluid ounces	1 quart	946ml /0.946 liters
8 pints	1 gallon/128 fluid ounces	4 quarts	3,785ml/3.78 liters
4 quarts	1 gallon/128 fluid ounces	1 gallon	3,785ml/3.78 liters
1.057 quarts			1,000ml/1 liter
1 gallon	4 quarts	128 fluid ounces	3,785ml/3.78 liters

Dry or weight measurements (approximate)

1 ounce		30 grams (28.35g)
2 ounces		55 grams
3 ounces		85 grams
4 ounces	¼ pound	125 grams
8 ounces	½ pound	240 grams
12 ounces	¾ pound	375 grams
16 ounces	1 pound	454 grams
32 ounces	2 pounds	907 grams
¼ pound	4 ounces	125 grams
½ pound	8 ounces	240 grams
¾ pound	12 ounces	375 grams
1 pound	16 ounces	454 grams
2 pounds	32 ounces	907 grams
2.2 pounds	35.2 ounces	1,000 grams/1 kilogram

Oven temperatures

250°F	130°C	Gas mark 1–2
300°F	150°C	Gas mark 2
350°F	180°C	Gas mark 4
375°F	190°C	Gas mark 5
400°F	200°C	Gas mark 6
425°F	220°C	Gas mark 7
450°F	230°C	Gas mark 8

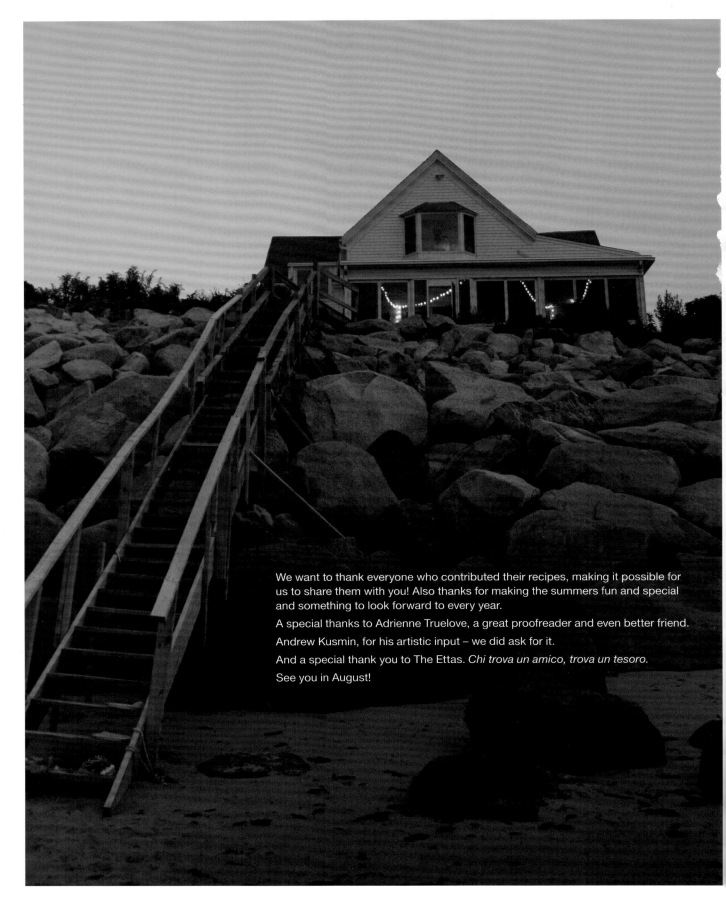

We want to thank everyone who contributed their recipes, making it possible for us to share them with you! Also thanks for making the summers fun and special and something to look forward to every year.

A special thanks to Adrienne Truelove, a great proofreader and even better friend.

Andrew Kusmin, for his artistic input – we did ask for it.

And a special thank you to The Ettas. *Chi trova un amico, trova un tesoro.*

See you in August!